CASSEROLE COOKING

SUPERCOOK'S KITCHEN

Marshall Cavendish London & New York

Picture Credit List

Theo Bergstrom 30
Delu/Paf International 4, 56
Alan Duns 14, 16, 18, 44, 48, 64, 66, 68, 94
Paul Kemp 8, 74
Don Last 34
Max Logan 88
David Meldrum 12, 20
Roger Phillips 6, 10, 22, 24, 26, 28, 36, 38,
    40, 46, 50, 54, 58, 60, 70, 72, 76, 80, 82,
    84, 86, 90, 92
Iain Reid 32, 52, 62

Recipes : Norma McMillan
House editor : Isabel Moore

Published by
Marshall Cavendish Books Limited
58 Old Compton Street
LONDON W1V 5PA

Printed in Great Britain

ISBN 0 85685 727 0

CONTENTS

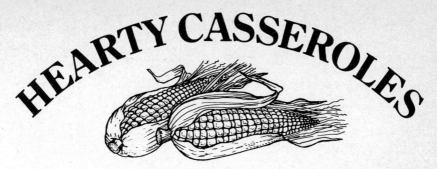

HEARTY CASSEROLES

Beef with corn & tomatoes

Metric/Imperial	American
1kg/2lb topside of beef, cubed	*2lb top round of beef, cubed*
60ml/4 tbs. paprika	*¼ cup paprika*
50g/2oz butter	*¼ cup butter*
2 medium onions, chopped	*2 medium onions, chopped*
2 garlic cloves, crushed	*2 garlic cloves, crushed*
250g/8oz canned tomatoes	*8oz canned tomatoes*
5ml/1 tsp. dried thyme	*1 tsp dried thyme*
1 bay leaf	*1 bay leaf*
2 carrots, sliced	*2 carrots, sliced*
200ml/⅓ pint white wine or stock	*1 cup white wine or stock*
½kg/1lb sweetcorn kernels	*1lb (3 cups) corn kernels*
150ml/¼ pint single cream	*⅔ cup light cream*
30ml/2 tbs. flour	*2 tbs. flour*

Preheat the oven to 180°C/350°F, Gas Mark 4.

Coat the beef cubes with the paprika. Melt the butter in a frying pan. Add the onions and garlic and fry until softened. Transfer to a casserole using a slotted spoon. Add the beef cubes to the pan, in batches, and fry until browned on all sides. Transfer the cubes to the casserole as they brown.

Add the undrained tomatoes, herbs and seasoning to taste, carrots and wine or stock to the pan and bring to the boil, stirring. Pour this mixture into the casserole and stir well. Cover the casserole and place it in the oven. Cook for 1 hour. Stir in the corn and cook for a further 20 minutes, covered.

Mix together the cream and flour. Stir into the mixture in the casserole. Re-cover and continue cooking for 20 minutes or until the beef cubes are tender. Serve hot. **SERVES 4**

Beef stew with chick peas

Metric/Imperial	American
3 bacon rashers, chopped	3 bacon slices, chopped
1½kg/3lb stewing steak, cubed	3lb chuck steak, cubed
30ml/2 tbs. oil	2 tbs. oil
2 large onions, thinly sliced	2 large onions, thinly sliced
2 garlic cloves, crushed	2 garlic cloves, crushed
15ml/1 tbs. flour	1 tbs. flour
1.2 litres/2 pints water	2½ pints water
30ml/2 tbs. tomato purée	2 tbs. tomato paste
350g/12oz tomatoes, skinned and quartered	¾lb tomatoes, skinned and quartered
5ml/1 tsp. dried basil	1 tsp. dried basil
175g/6oz canned and drained chick peas	1 cup canned and drained chick peas

Preheat the oven to 170°C/325°F, Gas Mark 3.

Fry the bacon in a frying pan until it is crisp and has rendered most of its fat. Transfer to a casserole, using a slotted spoon. Add the steak cubes to the pan, in batches, and fry until browned on all sides. Transfer the cubes to the casserole as they brown.

Add the oil to the frying pan. When it is hot, add the onions and garlic and fry until softened. Sprinkle over the flour and cook, stirring, until the flour is golden brown. Gradually stir in the water and bring to the boil, stirring. Stir in the tomato purée (paste), tomatoes, basil and seasoning to taste. Pour into the casserole, cover and place in the oven. Cook for 2 hours.

Add the chick peas, stir well and continue cooking for a further 30 minutes or until the meat is tender. Serve hot. **SERVES 6**

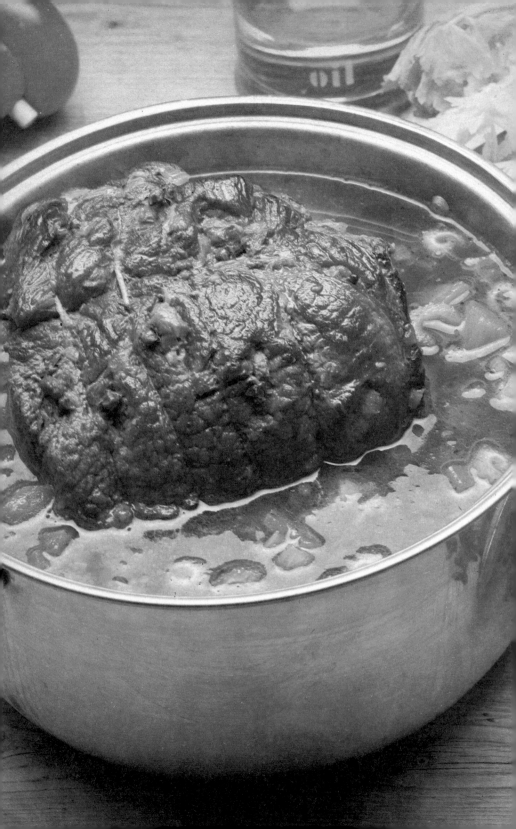

Beef & clove casserole

Metric/Imperial	American
1 garlic clove, crushed	*1 garlic clove, crushed*
5ml/1 tsp. dried marjoram	*1 tsp. dried marjoram*
25g/1oz salt pork	*1oz fatback*
1½kg/3lb lean topside of beef, in one piece	*3lb lean top round of beef, in one piece*
8 cloves	*8 cloves*
100g/4oz butter	*½ cup butter*
250ml/8fl oz red wine	*1 cup red wine*
250ml/8fl oz beef stock	*1 cup beef stock*
1 large onion, chopped	*1 large onion, chopped*
3 carrots, chopped	*3 carrots, chopped*
1 celery stalk, chopped	*1 celery stalk, chopped*

Mix together the garlic, marjoram and seasoning to taste. Cut the salt pork into thin strips and roll each strip in the garlic mixture. Make small incisions in the beef and insert the salt pork strips and the cloves.

Melt the butter in a saucepan. Add the beef and brown on all sides. Add the remaining ingredients with seasoning to taste and bring to the boil. Cover and simmer for 1¾ hours or until the beef is tender.

Transfer the beef to a warmed serving platter and remove the string used to tie it into shape. Slice and strain over some of the cooking juices. Serve hot.

SERVES 6

Flank steak stew with herbs

Metric/Imperial	American
40g/1½oz seasoned flour	6 tbs. seasoned flour
1½kg/3lb flank steak, cubed	3lb flank steak, cubed
75g/3oz butter	6 tbs. butter
30ml/2 tbs. oil	2 tbs. oil
2 medium onions, thinly sliced	2 medium onions, thinly sliced
1 garlic clove, crushed	1 garlic clove, crushed
1 large green pepper, cored, seeded and chopped	1 large green pepper, cored, seeded and chopped
50g/2oz walnuts, finely chopped	½ cup finely chopped walnuts
30ml/2 tbs. chopped parsley	2 tbs. chopped parsley
5ml/1 tsp. mixed herbs	1 tsp. mixed herbs
2 bay leaves	2 bay leaves
500ml/16fl oz beef stock	1 pint beef stock
30ml/2 tbs. tomato purée	2 tbs. tomato paste

Coat the beef cubes in all but 1 tablespoon of the seasoned flour. Melt half the butter with the oil in a saucepan. Add the beef cubes, in batches, and brown on all sides. Remove the cubes from the pan as they brown. Add 25g/1oz (2 tablespoons) of the remaining butter to the pan. When it has melted, add the onions, garlic and pepper and fry until the onions are softened. Stir in the walnuts, parsley, mixed herbs, bay leaves, stock, tomato purée (paste) and seasoning to taste and bring to the boil. Return the steak cubes to the pan, cover and simmer for 1½ hours or until the meat is tender.

Mix the reserved flour with the remaining butter to form a paste (beurre manié). Add this to the stew in small pieces, stirring, and simmer until thickened. Remove the bay leaves and serve hot.

SERVES 6

Beef with dumplings

Metric/Imperial	American
1kg/2lb stewing steak, cubed	2lb chuck steak, cubed
25g/1oz seasoned flour	$\frac{1}{4}$ cup seasoned flour
50g/2oz butter	4 tbs. butter
1 large onion, finely chopped	1 large onion, finely chopped
1.2 litres/2 pints beef stock	$2\frac{1}{2}$ pints beef stock
1 bay leaf	1 bay leaf
175g/6oz button mushrooms	6oz button mushrooms
150ml/$\frac{1}{4}$ pint soured cream	$\frac{2}{3}$ cup sour cream
DUMPLINGS	**DUMPLINGS**
250g/8oz fresh breadcrumbs	4 cups fresh breadcrumbs
60ml/4 tbs. water	$\frac{1}{4}$ cup water
3 eggs, beaten	3 eggs, beaten
22.5ml/$1\frac{1}{2}$ tbs. chopped parsley	$1\frac{1}{2}$ tbs. chopped parsley
1 onion, finely chopped	1 onion, finely chopped

Preheat the oven to 170°C/325°F, Gas Mark 3.

Coat the beef cubes in the seasoned flour. Melt the butter in a flame-proof casserole. Add the beef cubes, in batches, and brown on all sides. As the cubes brown, remove them from the casserole. Add the onion to the casserole and fry until softened. Return the beef to the casserole. Stir in the stock and bay leaf. Bring to the boil, cover and transfer to the oven. Cook for 2 hours.

Meanwhile, make the dumplings. Moisten the breadcrumbs with the water, and mix in the eggs, seasoning to taste, parsley and onion. With floured hands, shape the mixture into small dumplings.

Add the dumplings to the casserole with the mushrooms. Spoon the liquid over them, re-cover the casserole and continue cooking for 30 minutes. Remove the bay leaf and spoon over the sour cream before serving.

SERVES 4

Lamb with celery

Metric/Imperial	American
1kg/2lb lean lamb, cubed	2lb lean lamb, cubed
30ml/2 tbs. chopped fennel leaves	2 tbs. chopped fennel leaves
25g/1oz flour	¼ cup flour
60ml/4 tbs. oil	¼ cup oil
1 garlic clove, halved	1 garlic clove, halved
3 medium onions, thinly sliced into rings	3 medium onions, thinly sliced into rings
3 celery stalks, chopped	3 celery stalks, chopped
½kg/1lb okra, cut into 2.5cm/1in pieces	1lb okra, cut into 1 in pieces
45ml/3 tbs. chopped parsley	3 tbs. chopped parsley
250ml/8fl oz white wine or stock	1 cup white wine or stock
120ml/4fl oz soured cream	½ cup sour cream
120ml/4fl oz double cream	½ cup heavy cream
250ml/8fl oz tomato juice	1 cup tomato juice
7.5ml/1½ tsp. dried thyme	1½ tsp. dried thyme

Season the lamb cubes and rub with the fennel. Leave in a cool place for 1 hour. Coat the cubes with the flour.

Heat the oil with the garlic in a flameproof casserole. Discard the garlic. Add the lamb cubes, in batches, and fry until they are browned on all sides. Remove the cubes from the casserole as they brown. Add the onions to the casserole and fry until softened. Stir in the celery, okra, parsley and wine or stock and bring to the boil. Return the lamb cubes to the casserole, cover and simmer for 15 minutes.

Meanwhile, mix together the sour cream and double (heavy) cream. Stir the cream mixture into the casserole. Re-cover and cook gently for a further 20 minutes.

Preheat the oven to 170°C/325°F, Gas Mark 3.

Stir the tomato juice and thyme into the casserole. Re-cover and transfer to the oven. Cook for 30 to 45 minutes or until the lamb cubes are tender. Serve hot. **SERVES 4**

Lamb stew with vegetables

Metric/Imperial	American
2 small aubergines, cubed	2 small eggplants, cubed
50g/2oz seasoned flour	½ cup seasoned flour
1½kg/3lb boned lamb, cubed	3lb boneless lamb, cubed
2.5ml/½ tsp. grated nutmeg	½ tsp. grated nutmeg
2.5ml/½ tsp. dried mint	½ tsp. dried mint
2.5ml/½ tsp. turmeric	½ tsp. turmeric
45ml/3 tbs. oil	3 tbs. oil
2 onions, thinly sliced	2 onions, thinly sliced
4 large tomatoes, sliced	4 large tomatoes, sliced
250g/8oz courgettes, sliced	½lb zucchini, sliced
600ml/1 pint chicken stock	2½ cups chicken stock
2 large potatoes, peeled and cubed	2 large potatoes, peeled and cubed
200g/7oz canned chick peas, drained	7oz canned chick peas, drained

Put the aubergine (eggplant) cubes in a colander and sprinkle with salt. Leave for 30 minutes, then rinse and pat dry with paper towels. Preheat the oven to 180°C/350°F, Gas Mark 4. Coat the lamb cubes with the seasoned flour. Mix together the nutmeg, mint, turmeric and seasoning.

Heat the oil in a flameproof casserole. Add the lamb cubes, in batches, and fry until lightly browned on all sides. Remove the cubes from the pan as they brown. Add the onions to the casserole and fry until softened. Remove the casserole from the heat. Arrange the lamb, aubergines (eggplants), tomatoes and courgettes (zucchini) in the casserole in layers, sprinkling each layer with the spice mixture. Pour in the stock, cover and place the casserole in the oven. Cook for 1 hour.

Stir in the potatoes and chick peas. Return to the oven and continue to cook for 30 to 45 minutes or until tender. Serve hot. **SERVES 6**

Lamb casserole with leeks

Metric/Imperial	American
25g/1oz butter	2 tbs. butter
25g/1oz flour	¼ cup flour
600ml/1 pint milk	2½ cups milk
8 crushed peppercorns	8 crushed peppercorns
1.25ml/¼ tsp. paprika	¼ tsp. paprika
10ml/2 tsp. Worcestershire sauce	2 tsp. Worcestershire sauce
½kg/1lb shelled fresh peas	3 cups shelled fresh peas
2 medium leeks, chopped	2 medium leeks, chopped
1 celery stalk, chopped	1 celery stalk, chopped
2.5ml/½ tsp. dried sage	½ tsp. dried sage
½kg/1lb cooked lean lamb, diced	2 cups diced lean cooked lamb
30ml/2 tbs. chopped parsley	2 tbs. chopped parsley
45ml/3 tbs. wheat germ	3 tbs. wheat germ
50g/2oz grated cheese	½ cup grated cheese

Melt the butter in a flameproof casserole. Add the flour and cook, stirring, for 2 minutes. Gradually stir in the milk off the heat. Stir in the peppercorns, paprika and Worcestershire sauce and bring to the boil. Simmer until the sauce is smooth and thickened. Stir in the vegetables and sage and cook, stirring frequently, for 5 minutes. Add the lamb and cook gently for 15 minutes. Do not allow the mixture to boil.

Preheat the grill (broiler). Stir in the parsley and half the wheat germ. Remove the casserole from the heat and sprinkle the remaining wheat germ and cheese over the top. Place the casserole under the grill (broiler) and cook until the cheese has melted and the topping is golden brown. Serve hot. **SERVES 4**

Apple & pork casserole

Metric/Imperial	American
50g/2oz butter	¼ cup butter
1kg/2lb boned lean pork, cubed	2lb boneless lean pork, cubed
2 medium onions, chopped	2 medium onions, chopped
2.5ml/½ tsp. dried sage	½ tsp. dried sage
2 cooking apples, peeled, cored and thinly sliced	2 cooking apples, peeled, cored and thinly sliced
45ml/3 tbs. water	3 tbs. water
¾kg/1½lb potatoes, peeled	1½lb potatoes, peeled
30ml/2 tbs hot milk	2 tbs. hot milk

Preheat the oven to 170°C/325°F, Gas Mark 3.

Grease a casserole with 15g/½oz (1 tablespoon) of the butter. Put about one-third of the pork cubes in the casserole. Mix together the onions, sage and seasoning to taste and sprinkle about half of this over the pork. Cover with half the apple slices. Continue making layers in this way, finishing with pork. Sprinkle over the water. Cover the casserole and place it in the oven. Cook for 2 to 2½ hours or until the pork is tender.

Thirty minutes before the casserole is ready, cook the potatoes in boiling salted water until they are tender. Drain well and mash with the milk and 25g/1oz (2 tablespoons) of the remaining butter. Spread the mashed potatoes over the pork mixture. Cut the remaining butter into small pieces and dot over the potato. Return to the oven and cook for a further 15 minutes or until the top of the potato layer is golden brown. Serve hot.   **SERVES 4**

Southern sparerib (boston blade)

Metric/Imperial	American
1 x 1½kg/3lb pork spare rib joint, boned, rolled, cut into four and each piece halved lengthways	3lb boneless pork Boston blade roast, rolled, cut into four and each piece halved lengthwise
50g/2oz seasoned flour	½ cup seasoned flour
30ml/2 tbs. oil	2 tbs. oil
450ml/¾ pint dry cider	1 pint hard cider
GARNISH	**GARNISH**
30ml/2 tbs. olive oil	2 tbs. olive oil
2 garlic cloves, crushed	2 garlic cloves, crushed
1 large onion, thinly sliced	1 large onion, thinly sliced
1 large green pepper, cored, seeded and sliced	1 large green pepper, cored, seeded and sliced
250g/8oz courgettes, sliced	½lb zucchini, sliced
½kg/1lb tomatoes, skinned, seeded and chopped	1lb tomatoes, skinned, seeded and chopped
250ml/8fl oz chicken stock	1 cup chicken stock
15ml/1 tbs. tomato purée	1 tbs. tomato paste
1 bay leaf	1 bay leaf

Preheat the oven to 180°C/350°F, Gas Mark 4.

Coat the meat with the seasoned flour. Heat the oil in a flameproof casserole. Add the pork pieces and brown on all sides. Pour in the cider and bring to the boil. Cover and transfer the casserole to the oven. Cook for 1 to 1¼ hours or until the meat is tender.

Meanwhile, make the garnish. Heat the oil in a frying pan. Add the garlic and onion and fry until softened. Add the pepper and courgettes (zucchini) and cook for a further 3 minutes. Stir in the remaining ingredients and bring to the boil. Simmer for 15 to 20 minutes or until all the vegetables are tender. Remove the bay leaf.

Drain the pork pieces and arrange them in a warmed serving dish. Spoon around the garnish and serve.

SERVES 4

White meat casserole

Metric/Imperial	American
50g/2oz butter	¼ cup butter
1 medium onion, finely chopped	1 medium onion, finely chopped
1½kg/3lb stewing veal, cubed	3lb veal stew meat, cubed
298g/10½oz canned condensed cream of mushroom soup	10½oz canned condensed cream of mushroom soup
250ml/8fl oz milk	1 cup milk
5ml/1 tsp. paprika	1 tsp. paprika
1.25ml/¼ tsp grated nutmeg	¼ tsp. grated nutmeg
250g/8oz button mushrooms, halved	½lb button mushrooms, halved

Preheat the oven to 180°C/350°F, Gas Mark 4.

Melt half the butter in a flameproof casserole. Add the onion and fry until softened. Add the veal cubes and fry until they are lightly browned on all sides. Mix the soup with the milk and add to the casserole with the paprika, nutmeg and seasoning to taste. Cover the casserole and transfer it to the oven. Cook for 2 hours.

Melt the remaining butter in a saucepan. Add the mushrooms, cover and cook until they are just tender. Add the mushrooms to the casserole and stir well. Re-cover and cook for a further 30 minutes or until the veal is tender.

SERVES 6

Quick cassoulet

Metric/Imperial	American
50g/2oz pork fat, finely diced	2oz pork fatback, finely diced
½kg/1lb pie veal, cubed	1lb veal stew meat, cubed
250g/8oz boned blade of pork, cubed	½lb boneless pork blade steak, cubed
350g/12oz German sausage, thickly sliced	¾lb German sausage, thickly sliced
175g/6oz garlic sausage, sliced	6oz garlic sausage, sliced
10 garlic cloves	10 garlic cloves
400g/14oz canned tomatoes	14oz canned tomatoes
15ml/1 tbs. tomato purée	1 tbs. tomato paste
1kg/2lb canned haricot beans, drained	2lb canned navy beans, drained
1 bouquet garni	1 bouquet garni
275g/10oz canned carrots, drained	10oz canned carrots, drained
5ml/1 tsp. paprika	1 tsp. paprika
175ml/6fl oz red wine or stock	¾ cup red wine or stock

Preheat the oven to 190°C/375°F, Gas Mark 5.

Fry the pork fat in a flameproof casserole until it has rendered some of its fat and the dice are crispy. Add the veal, pork and sausages and fry until browned on all sides. Stir in the garlic, undrained tomatoes, tomato purée (paste), beans and bouquet garni. Cover the casserole and transfer to the oven. Cook for 30 minutes.

Remove the bouquet garni from the casserole and add the carrots, paprika and wine or stock. Stir well, re-cover and continue cooking for 20 minutes. Serve hot. **SERVES 8**

Liver Italian-style

Metric/Imperial	American
100g/4oz butter	½ cup butter
2 shallots, finely chopped	2 shallots, finely chopped
2 garlic cloves, crushed	2 garlic cloves, crushed
6 spring onions, finely chopped	6 scallions, finely chopped
125g/4oz mushrooms, sliced	¼lb mushrooms, sliced
¾kg/1½lb lamb's liver, thickly sliced and cut into 7.5cm/3in pieces	1½lb lamb liver, thickly sliced and cut into 3in pieces
400g/14oz canned tomatoes, chopped	14oz canned tomatoes, chopped
30ml/2 tbs. tomato purée	2 tbs. tomato paste
120ml/4fl oz beef stock	½ cup beef stock
7.5ml/1½ tsp. wine vinegar	1½ tsp. wine vinegar
5ml/1 tsp. dried basil	1 tsp. dried basil
15ml/1 tbs. chopped parsley	1 tbs. chopped parsley

Preheat the oven to 180°C/350°F, Gas Mark 4.

Melt half the butter in a frying pan. Add the shallots, garlic and spring onions (scallions) and fry until softened. Add the mushrooms and fry until they are lightly browned. Transfer the mushroom mixture to a casserole. Add the remaining butter to the pan. When it has melted, add the liver in batches, and fry until browned on all sides. Transfer the pieces to the casserole as they brown.

Add the undrained tomatoes, tomato purée (paste), stock and vinegar to the frying pan and bring to the boil, stirring. Stir in seasoning to taste and the remaining ingredients. Stir this mixture into the casserole. Transfer to the oven and cook 30 to 45 minutes or until the liver is tender. Serve hot.

SERVES 4

Chicken with beans & corn

Metric/Imperial	American
8 chicken pieces	8 chicken pieces
50g/2oz butter	$\frac{1}{4}$ cup butter
175g/6oz French beans	$\frac{3}{4}$ cup green beans
250g/8oz sweetcorn kernels	$1\frac{1}{2}$ cups corn kernels
MARINADE	**MARINADE**
250ml/8fl oz orange juice	1 cup orange juice
grated rind of 1 large orange	grated rind of 1 large orange
2 garlic cloves, crushed	2 garlic cloves, crushed
2 shallots, finely chopped	2 shallots, finely chopped
2.5ml/$\frac{1}{2}$ tsp ground cumin	$\frac{1}{2}$ tsp. ground cumin
1.25ml/$\frac{1}{4}$ tsp. ground allspice	$\frac{1}{4}$ tsp. ground allspice
1.25ml/$\frac{1}{4}$ tsp. mild chilli powder	$\frac{1}{4}$ tsp. mild chili powder

Mix together the ingredients for the marinade with seasoning to taste. Add the chicken pieces and leave to marinate for 8 hours, stirring occasionally. Remove the chicken pieces from the marinade and pat dry with paper towels. Reserve the marinade.

Preheat the oven to 180°C/350°F, Gas Mark 4.

Melt the butter in a flameproof casserole. Add the chicken pieces, in batches, and brown on all sides. Return all the chicken pieces to the pot and add the beans, corn and reserved marinade. Bring to the boil, then cover and transfer to the oven. Cook for 1 hour or until the chicken pieces are tender. Serve hot.   **SERVES 4**

Hare stew

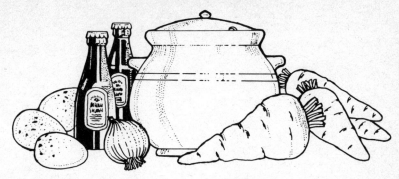

Metric/Imperial

1 x 2½kg/5lb hare, cut into
  serving pieces
50g/2oz seasoned flour
60ml/4 tbs. oil
175g/6oz pickling onions
2 garlic cloves, halved
1 parsnip, quartered
6 small turnips
250g/8oz red cabbage, shredded
300ml/½ pint chicken stock

MARINADE

1 bottle dry white wine
1 large onion, sliced
15ml/1 tbs. peppercorns
5ml/1 tsp. paprika
30ml/2 tbs. olive oil

American

1 x 5lb hare, cut up into
  serving pieces
½ cup seasoned flour
¼ cup oil
6oz pearl onions
2 garlic cloves, halved
1 parsnip, quartered
6 small turnips
½lb red cabbage, shredded
1¼ cups chicken stock

MARINADE

1 bottle dry white wine
1 large onion, sliced
1 tbs. peppercorns
1 tsp. paprika
2 tbs. olive oil

Mix together the marinade ingredients. Add the hare pieces and leave to marinate for 24 hours, turning occasionally. Remove the hare pieces from the marinade and pat dry with paper towels. Strain the marinade and reserve. Coat the hare pieces with the seasoned flour.
Heat the oil in a saucepan. Add the hare pieces, in batches, and brown on all sides. Return the hare pieces to the pan and add the onions, garlic, parsnip, turnips, cabbage, stock and reserved marinade. Bring to the boil, cover and simmer for 3 to 4 hours or until the hare pieces are very tender. Serve hot. **SERVES 8**

Sausage & lentil casserole

Metric/Imperial	American
½kg/1lb lentils	2 cups lentils
1.2 litres/2 pints beef stock	2½ pints beef stock
1 large onion, halved	1 large onion, halved
1 bouquet garni	1 bouquet garni
25g/1oz butter	2 tbs. butter
6 bacon rashers, chopped	6 bacon slices, chopped
2 garlic cloves, chopped	2 garlic cloves, chopped
6 large sausages (such as knackwurst), sliced	6 large sausages (such as knackwurst), sliced
100g/4oz Cheddar cheese, grated	1 cup grated Cheddar cheese

Put the lentils in a saucepan and pour over the stock. Add the onion, bouquet garni and 5ml/1 teaspoon salt. Bring to the boil, then simmer for 1 hour or until the lentils are tender. Drain the lentils, reserving the liquid. Discard the onion and bouquet garni.

Preheat the oven to 180°C/350°F, Gas Mark 4.

Melt the butter in a frying pan. Add the bacon and garlic and fry until the bacon is crisp. Add the sausages and fry for a further 5 minutes, stirring occasionally. Remove from the heat.

Make a layer of half the lentils in a casserole. Cover with the sausages and bacon mixture and sprinkle with pepper. Top with the remaining lentils and pour in the lentil cooking liquid. Sprinkle the cheese over the top and place in the oven. Cook for 1 hour or until the ingredients are piping hot and the cheese is golden brown. Serve hot.

SERVES 6

Kidney bean & bacon casserole

Metric/Imperial

250g/8oz bacon, diced
1 large onion, finely chopped
2 garlic cloves, crushed
1 large red pepper, cored, seeded and
  thinly sliced
4 celery stalks, cut into 5cm/2 in
  pieces
250g/8oz tomatoes, skinned, seeded
  and chopped
1 bouquet garni
400g/14oz canned red kidney beans,
  drained
30ml/2 tbs. chopped parsley
30ml/2 tbs. chopped chives
50g/2oz Parmesan cheese, grated

American

½lb bacon, diced
1 large onion, finely chopped
2 garlic cloves, crushed
1 large red pepper, cored, seeded and
  thinly sliced
4 celery stalks, cut into 2 in
  pieces
½lb tomatoes, skinned, seeded and
  chopped
1 bouquet garni
14oz canned red kidney beans,
  drained
2 tbs. chopped parsley
2 tbs. chopped chives
½ cup grated Parmesan cheese

Fry the bacon in a saucepan until it is crisp and has rendered most of its fat. Add the onion, garlic, pepper and celery and fry until the onion is softened. Stir in the tomatoes, bouquet garni and seasoning to taste. Cover and cook for 30 minutes. Stir in the beans, parsley and chives and cook, covered, for a further 15 minutes. Serve hot, sprinkled with the Parmesan. **SERVES 4**

Braised celery with bacon

Metric/Imperial	American
2 small bunches of celery	*2 small heads of celery*
100g/4oz bacon rashers	*¼lb bacon slices*
1 small carrot, sliced	*1 small carrot, sliced*
1 onion, sliced	*1 onion, sliced*
1 bouquet garni	*1 bouquet garni*
900ml/1½ pints boiling chicken stock	*3¾ cups boiling chicken stock*

Preheat the oven to 180°C/350°F, Gas Mark 4.

Blanch the celery stalks in boiling water for 1 minute. Drain. Lay the bacon on the bottom of a casserole. Put in the sliced carrot and onion and place the celery on top. Add the bouquet garni and seasoning to taste and pour in the stock. Cover the casserole and place it in the oven. Cook for 1½ hours. Uncover the casserole and continue cooking for 30 minutes at 200°C/400°F, Gas Mark 6.

Remove the celery from the casserole. Halve the stalks and arrange them in a warmed serving dish. Keep warm. Strain the cooking liquid into a saucepan and boil to reduce. If necessary, thicken the liquid with a little beurre manié (made with 1 tablespoon each of flour and butter mixed to a paste). Pour the liquid over the celery and serve.

SERVES 4

Barley & mushroom casserole

Metric/Imperial	American
30ml/2 tbs. oil	2 tbs. oil
3 large onions, thinly sliced	3 large onions, thinly sliced
350g/12oz mushrooms, sliced	¾lb mushrooms, sliced
350g/12oz pearl barley	1⅔ cups pearl barley
900g/1lb 14 oz canned tomatoes	1lb 14oz canned tomatoes
175ml/6fl oz chicken stock	¾ cup chicken stock
2 green peppers, cored, seeded and sliced	2 green peppers, cored, seeded and sliced
10ml/2 tsp. chopped thyme	2 tsp. chopped thyme
30ml/2 tbs. chopped parsley	2 tbs. chopped parsley

Preheat the oven to 180°C/350°F, Gas Mark 4.

Heat the oil in a frying pan. Add the onions and fry until softened. Add the mushrooms and fry for a further 2 minutes.

Put the barley in a casserole and stir in the onions and mushrooms. Stir in the undrained tomatoes, stock, peppers, thyme and seasoning to taste. Cover and place in the oven. Cook for 1 hour or until the barley is tender and most of the liquid has been absorbed. Serve hot, sprinkled with parsley.

SERVES 6

Oven-braised beef

Metric/Imperial	American
1½kg/3lb stewing beef, cubed	3lb chuck steak, cubed
75g/3oz seasoned flour	¾ cup seasoned flour
75g/3oz butter	6 tbs. butter
6 medium onions, thinly sliced	6 medium onions, thinly sliced
6 carrots, chopped	6 carrots, chopped
350ml/12fl oz red wine	1½ cups red wine
5ml/1 tsp. grated lemon rind	1 tsp. grated lemon rind
5ml/1 tsp. dried oregano	1 tsp. dried oregano

Preheat the oven to 170°C/325°F, Gas Mark 3.

Coat the beef cubes with the seasoned flour.

Melt 50g/2oz (¼ cup) of the butter in a flameproof casserole. Add the beef cubes, in batches, and fry until they are browned on all sides. Remove the cubes from the pan as they brown. Add the remaining butter to the casserole. When it has melted, add the onions and fry until softened. Add the carrots and fry until they are lightly browned. Stir in the remaining ingredients with seasoning to taste and bring to the boil.

Return the beef cubes to the casserole. Cover and transfer to the oven. Cook for 2 to 2½ hours or until the beef cubes are tender. Serve hot.   **SERVES 6**

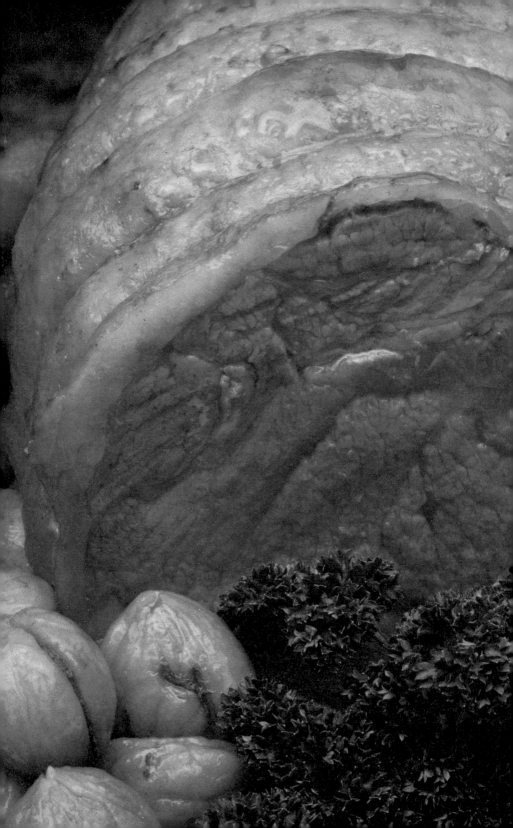

Braised beef with sausages

Metric/Imperial	American
22.5ml/1½ tbs. oil	1½ tbs. oil
1 x 1¾-2kg/3½-4lb boned and rolled sirloin of beef	1 x 3½-4lb beef tenderloin tip roast
1 carrot, sliced	1 carrot, sliced
1 small onion, sliced	1 small onion, sliced
1 bay leaf	1 bay leaf
½kg/1lb chipolata sausages	1lb pork link sausages
½kg/1lb pickling onions	1lb pearl onions
22.5ml/1½ tbs. butter	1½ tbs. butter
5ml/1 tsp. sugar	1 tsp. sugar
300ml/½ pint beef stock	1¼ cups beef stock
7.5ml/1½ tsp. flour	1½ tsp. flour

Preheat the oven to 190°C/375°F, Gas Mark 5.
Heat the oil in a flameproof casserole. Put in the beef and brown lightly on all sides. Remove the beef from the casserole. Add the vegetables to the casserole and fry until lightly browned. Add the bay leaf and seasoning to taste. Put the beef on top of the vegetables, cover and transfer to the oven. Cook for 50 minutes for rare beef. Turn and baste the meat at least twice during cooking.
Meanwhile grill (broil) or fry the sausages. Drain and keep warm.
Parboil the onions for 1 minute, then drain. Return the cleaned-out pan to the heat and add 15ml/1 tablespoon of the butter. When it has melted stir in the sugar, seasoning to taste and onions. Cook gently for 10 minutes or until the onions are tender and glazed.
Transfer the beef to a carving board. Skim the fat from the cooking juices and strain into a saucepan. Stir in the stock and bring to the boil. Boil for 4 minutes. Mix the remaining butter with the flour to make a paste (beurre manié). Add this in small pieces to the cooking liquid, stirring, and simmer until thickened.
Carve the beef in thick slices and garnish with the sausages and onions. Serve with the sauce. **SERVES 6-8**

Braised beef with brandy & wine

Metric/Imperial	American
60ml/4 tbs. oil	*¼ cup oil*
1 x 2.5kg/5lb topside of beef, rolled and tied	*1 x 5lb top round of beef, rolled and tied*
2 large onions, sliced	*2 large onions, sliced*
2 carrots, sliced	*2 carrots, sliced*
2 garlic cloves, crushed	*2 garlic cloves, crushed*
120ml/4fl oz brandy	*½ cup brandy*
300ml/½ pint dry red wine	*1¼ cups dry red wine*
4 bacon rashers, chopped	*4 bacon slices, chopped*
1 bouquet garni	*1 bouquet garni*
3 tomatoes, halved	*3 tomatoes, halved*

Preheat the oven to 150°C/300°F, Gas Mark 2.

Heat the oil in a flameproof casserole. Put in the beef and brown on all sides. Add the onions, carrots and garlic and cook for a further 5 minutes. Stir in the brandy, wine, bacon, bouquet garni and seasoning to taste and bring to the boil. Cover the casserole and transfer it to the oven. Cook for 4 hours or until the meat is very tender.

Transfer the beef to a warmed serving platter. Strain the cooking liquid and skim off all the fat. Serve the beef garnished with the tomatoes and the cooking liquid as a sauce. **SERVES 8**

Country-style lamb

Metric/Imperial	American
1 x 1kg/2lb best end of lamb, chine bone removed	*1 x 2lb lamb rib roast, chine bone removed*
25g/1oz butter	*2 tbs. butter*
45ml/3 tbs. oil	*3 tbs. oil*
1 cooking apple, peeled, cored and chopped	*1 cooking apple, peeled, cored and chopped*
3 medium potatoes, sliced	*3 medium potatoes, sliced*
1 medium onion, thinly sliced	*1 medium onion, thinly sliced*
175ml/6fl oz beef stock	*¾ cup beef stock*
10ml/2 tsp. tomato purée	*2 tsp. tomato paste*
2.5ml/½ tsp. dried marjoram	*½ tsp. dried marjoram*

Preheat the oven to 190°C/375°F, Gas Mark 5.

Cut the flap of bones from the lamb (or have the butcher do this for you) and remove the strips of meat from between the bones. Melt the butter with 15ml/1 tablespoon of the oil in a roasting pan. Put the meat, including the strips of meat, and apple into the pan and place in the oven. Roast for 30 minutes, turning occasionally.

Meanwhile, heat the remaining oil in a frying pan. Add the potato and onion slices and fry for 10 minutes or until the potatoes are lightly browned. Remove from the heat.

Remove the meat from the oven and cut between the bones into chops. Make a layer of about a third of the potato and onion slices in a casserole. Put half the chops on top. Cover with another third of the potato and onion slices and put the remaining chops, meat strips and apple on top. Pour over the juices from the roasting pan and cover with the remaining potato and onion slices.

Mix together the stock, tomato purée (paste), marjoram and seasoning to taste and pour into the casserole. Cover and place in the oven. Cook for 15 minutes.

SERVES 3-4

Italian braised lamb

Metric/Imperial	American
1kg/2lb boned shoulder of lamb, trimmed and cubed	2lb boned shoulder of lamb, trimmed and cubed
25g/1oz seasoned flour	¼ cup seasoned flour
2 bacon rashers, diced	2 bacon slices, diced
30ml/2 tbs. oil	2 tbs. oil
1 onion, finely chopped	1 onion, finely chopped
1 garlic clove, crushed	1 garlic clove, crushed
250g/8oz canned tomatoes	8oz canned tomatoes
600ml/1 pint beef stock	2½ cups beef stock
1 bay leaf	1 bay leaf
5ml/1 tsp. dried oregano	1 tsp. dried oregano
3 egg yolks	3 egg yolks
30ml/2 tbs. lemon juice	2 tbs. lemon juice

Preheat the oven to 180°C/350°F, Gas Mark 4.

Coat the lamb cubes with the seasoned flour. Put the bacon in a frying pan and fry until it is crisp and has rendered most of its fat. Remove from the pan with a slotted spoon and place in a casserole. Add the oil to the pan. When it is hot, add the lamb, in batches, and fry until it is browned on all sides. As the cubes brown, transfer them to the casserole. Add the onion and garlic to the pan and fry until softened. Stir in the undrained tomatoes, stock, bay leaf, oregano and seasoning to taste and bring to the boil. Stir into the casserole, cover and place in the oven. Cook for 1¾ hours or until the meat is tender.

Transfer the lamb cubes to a warmed serving dish, using a slotted spoon. Keep warm. Strain the cooking liquid into a saucepan. Skim any fat from the surface.

Mix together the egg yolks and lemon juice and stir in about 45ml/3 tablespoons of the cooking liquid. Whisk this egg mixture into the remaining cooking liquid. Cook gently, stirring, until the sauce thickens enough to coat the back of the spoon. Do not let the sauce boil or it will curdle. Pour the sauce over the lamb and serve hot.

SERVES 4

Cabbage & lamb hotpot

Metric/Imperial

15g/½oz butter
4 large lamb chops
1 medium green cabbage, shredded
2.5ml/½ tsp. dried rosemary
150g/5oz tomato purée
60ml/4 tbs. water

American

1 tbs. butter
4 large lamb chops
1 medium green cabbage, shredded
½ tsp. dried rosemary
½ cup tomato paste
¼ cup water

Preheat the oven to 180°C/350°F, Gas Mark 4.
Melt the butter in a flameproof casserole. Add the chops and brown on both sides. Remove the chops from the casserole.
Add the remaining ingredients to the casserole with seasoning to taste and mix well. Return the chops to the casserole and bury them in the cabbage mixture. Cover the casserole and transfer it to the oven. Cook for 45 minutes or until the meat is tender. Serve hot. **SERVES 4**

Braised neck of veal

Metric/Imperial	American
1 x 2kg/4lb best end of neck of veal, chine bone removed	1 x 4lb veal rib roast, chine bone bone removed
1.25ml/¼ tsp. ground cloves	¼ tsp. ground cloves
1.25ml/¼ tsp. ground mace	¼ tsp. ground mace
4 bacon rashers	4 bacon slices
1 medium onion, finely chopped	1 medium onion, finely chopped
1 large carrot, sliced	1 large carrot, sliced
2 celery stalks, chopped	2 celery stalks, chopped
1 bouquet garni	1 bouquet garni
6 black peppercorns	6 black peppercorns
350ml/12fl oz chicken stock	1½ cups chicken stock
15ml/1 tbs. lemon juice	1 tbs. lemon juice

Preheat the oven to 180°C/350°F, Gas Mark 4.

Cut off the short pieces of rib bone from the flap on the veal, or have your butcher do this for you. Rub the meat all over with seasoning, the cloves and mace.

Fry the bacon in a flameproof casserole until it is crisp and has rendered its fat. Discard the bacon. Add the vegetables to the casserole and fry until the onion is softened. Stir in the bouquet garni, peppercorns, stock and lemon juice. Put the veal on top and bring to the boil. Cover and transfer the casserole to the oven. Cook for 2 hours or until the veal is tender. Uncover and continue cooking for a further 20 minutes.

Transfer the veal to a warmed serving dish. Skim the fat from the cooking liquid and strain over the meat. **SERVES 4-6**

Braised oxtail with celery

Metric/Imperial	American
2 oxtails, cut into pieces	2 oxtails, cut into pieces
50g/2oz seasoned flour	½ cup seasoned flour
75ml/5 tbs. olive oil	5 tbs. olive oil
1 large onion, finely chopped	1 large onion, finely chopped
2 garlic cloves, finely chopped	2 garlic cloves, finely chopped
450ml/15fl oz beef stock	2 cups beef stock
400g/14oz canned tomatoes, drained and chopped	14oz canned tomatoes, drained and chopped
30ml/2 tbs. tomato purée	2 tbs. tomato paste
1 bouquet garni	1 bouquet garni
1 bunch of celery, chopped	1 head of celery, chopped
10ml/2 tsp. cornflour	2 tsp. cornstarch
15ml/1 tbs. cold water	1 tbs. cold water

Preheat the oven to 170°C/325°F, Gas Mark 3.
Coat the oxtail pieces with the seasoned flour. Heat half the oil in a frying pan. Add the oxtail pieces, in batches, and brown on all sides. Remove the oxtail pieces as they brown and place them in a flame-proof casserole. Add the remaining oil to the frying pan. When it is hot, add the onion and garlic and fry until softened. Stir in the stock and return to the boil. Boil until reduced by a quarter. Pour over the oxtail pieces, then mix in the tomatoes, tomato purée (paste) and bouquet garni. Cover and place in the oven. Cook for 3½ hours.
Blanch the celery in boiling water for 5 minutes. Drain well and add to the casserole. Re-cover and continue cooking for 30 minutes. Skim any fat from the surface of the oxtail mixture. Discard the bouquet garni. Dissolve the cornflour in the water and add to the casserole. Stir well and simmer on top of the stove until the liquid thickens slightly. Serve hot.

SERVES 6

Mexican pork & rice

Metric/Imperial	American
30ml/2 tbs. oil	2 tbs. oil
1 medium onion, chopped	1 medium onion, chopped
¾kg/1½lb minced pork	1½lb ground pork
2 celery stalks, chopped	2 celery stalks, chopped
1 small green pepper, cored, seeded and cut into rings	1 small green pepper, cored, seeded and cut into rings
75g/3oz sultanas	½ cup seedless white raisins
1 garlic clove, crushed	1 garlic clove, crushed
1.25ml/¼ tsp. ground cumin	¼ tsp. ground cumin
2.5ml/½ tsp. hot chilli powder	½ tsp. hot chilli powder
15ml/1 tbs. chopped parsley	1 tbs. chopped parsley
175g/6oz long-grain rice	1 cup long-grain rice
400g/14oz canned tomatoes	14oz canned tomatoes
120ml/4fl oz water	½ cup water
30ml/2 tbs. tomato purée	2 tbs. tomato paste
juice of ½ lemon	juice of ½ lemon
45ml/3 tbs. pine nuts	3 tbs. pine nuts

Preheat the oven to 180°C/350°F, Gas Mark 4.
Heat the oil in a flameproof casserole. Add the onion and fry until softened. Add the pork and fry until the meat loses its pinkness. Stir in the celery, pepper, sultanas (raisins), garlic, cumin, chilli powder, parsley, seasoning to taste and rice. Fry for 5 minutes, stirring, until the rice has changed colour. Stir in the undrained tomatoes, water and tomato purée (paste). Bring to the boil, cover and simmer for 15 minutes. Transfer to the oven and cook for 25 minutes.
Uncover and sprinkle over the lemon juice and pine nuts. Return the casserole to the oven and cook for a further 10 minutes. **SERVES 4**

Beef stew with rice & tomatoes

Metric/Imperial	American
30ml/2 tbs. olive oil	*2 tbs. olive oil*
2 bacon rashers, diced	*2 bacon slices, diced*
1½kg/3lb stewing steak, cubed	*3lb chuck steak, cubed*
2 medium onions, sliced	*2 medium onions, sliced*
250g/8oz long-grain rice	*1⅓ cups long-grain rice*
300ml/½ pint dry white wine	*1¼ cups dry white wine*
450ml/¾ pint beef stock	*1 pint beef stock*
2 garlic cloves, crushed	*2 garlic cloves, crushed*
2.5ml/½ tsp. dried thyme	*½ tsp. dried thyme*
pinch of powdered saffron	*pinch of powdered saffron*
½kg/1lb ripe tomatoes, skinned,	*1lb ripe tomatoes, skinned, seeded*
seeded and chopped	*and chopped*
100g/4oz grated cheese	*1 cup grated cheese*

Preheat the oven to 170°C/325°F, Gas Mark 3.
Heat the oil in a frying pan and fry the bacon until it is browned. Transfer to a casserole, using a slotted spoon. Add the beef cubes to the frying pan, in batches, and brown on all sides. As the cubes of beef brown, transfer them to the casserole. Add the onions to the pan and fry until softened. Transfer to the casserole. Add the rice to the pan and cook, stirring, until it looks milky. Transfer the rice to a bowl.

Add the wine to the frying pan and stir well to mix with the sediment in the pan, then stir in the stock, seasoning to taste, garlic, thyme and saffron. Bring to the boil and pour into the casserole. Stir, cover and place in the oven. Cook for 1 hour. Stir in the tomatoes, re-cover and continue cooking for 2 hours or until the meat is tender.

Increase the oven temperature to 190°C/375°F, Gas Mark 5. Stir the rice into the casserole, re-cover and continue to cook for 20 minutes or until the rice is tender and the liquid absorbed. Adjust the seasoning, stir in the cheese and serve hot. **SERVES 6-8**

Veal & rice casserole

Metric/Imperial	American
50g/2oz butter	¼ cup butter
1kg/2lb pie veal, cubed	2lb veal stew meat, cubed
2 medium onions, finely chopped	2 medium onions, finely chopped
30ml/2 tbs. paprika	2 tbs. paprika
600ml/1 pint chicken stock	2½ cups chicken stock
5ml/1 tsp. dried thyme	1 tsp. dried thyme
300g/10oz long-grain rice	1⅔ cups long-grain rice

Melt the butter in a saucepan. Add the veal cubes and onions and fry until the veal cubes are lightly browned on all sides and the onions are softened. Stir in the paprika, then stir in the stock, seasoning to taste and thyme. Bring to the boil, cover and simmer for 1¼ hours. Stir in the rice. Re-cover the pan and simmer for a further 20 to 25 minutes or until the rice is cooked and has absorbed all the liquid. Serve hot.

SERVES 4

Chicken with rice

Metric/Imperial	American
8 chicken pieces	8 chicken pieces
25g/1oz seasoned flour	¼ cup seasoned flour
6 bacon rashers, diced	6 bacon slices, diced
2 onions, chopped	2 onions, chopped
1 garlic clove, crushed	1 garlic clove, crushed
400g/14oz canned tomatoes	14oz canned tomatoes
75g/3oz canned pimientos, drained	3oz canned pimientos, drained
10ml/2 tsp. paprika	2 tsp. paprika
1.25ml/¼ tsp. powdered saffron	¼ tsp. powdered saffron
600ml/1 pint water	2½ cups water
250g/8oz long-grain rice	1⅓ cups long-grain rice
175g/6oz frozen peas	1 cup frozen peas
30ml/2 tbs. chopped parsley	2 tbs. chopped parsley

Preheat the oven to 180°C/350°F, Gas Mark 4.

Coat the chicken pieces with the seasoned flour. Fry the bacon in a flameproof casserole until it is crisp and has rendered its fat. Add the chicken pieces and brown on all sides in the bacon fat. Remove the chicken pieces from the casserole. Add the onions and garlic to the casserole and fry until softened. Return the chicken pieces and add the undrained tomatoes, pimientos, paprika, saffron, seasoning to taste and water. Bring to the boil, then stir in the rice.

Cover the casserole and transfer it to the oven. Cook for 30 minutes. Add the peas and cook for a further 10 minutes or until the chicken is tender. Serve sprinkled with the parsley. **SERVES 4**

Chicken liver risotto

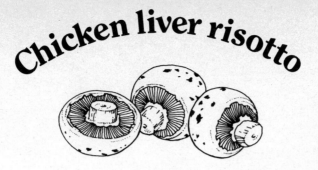

Metric/Imperial	American
50g/2oz butter	¼ cup butter
1 onion, finely chopped	1 onion, finely chopped
100g/4oz mushrooms, sliced	¼lb mushrooms, sliced
300g/10oz long-grain rice	1⅔ cups long-grain rice
600ml/1 pint boiling chicken stock	2½ cups boiling chicken stock
8 chicken livers, chopped	8 chicken livers, chopped
30ml/2 tbs. chopped parsley	2 tbs. chopped parsley
50g/2oz Parmesan cheese, grated	½ cup grated Parmesan cheese

Melt three-quarters of the butter in a saucepan. Add the onion and fry until softened. Stir in the mushrooms and fry for a further 3 minutes. Stir in the rice and cook, stirring, for 2 minutes, then stir in the stock. Cover and simmer gently for 20 minutes or until the rice is tender and has absorbed all the stock.

Meanwhile, melt the remaining butter in another pan. Add the chicken livers and fry for 10 minutes, stirring occasionally.

Stir the chicken livers into the rice mixture with the parsley. Serve hot, sprinkled with the Parmesan.

SERVES 4

Long Island seafood pilau

Metric/Imperial

50g/2oz butter
1 large onion, chopped
1 garlic clove, crushed
1 green pepper, cored, seeded and
  chopped
1 red pepper, cored, seeded and
  chopped
4 medium tomatoes, skinned, seeded
  and chopped
2.5ml/½ tsp. cayenne
250g/8oz peeled shrimps
24 oysters, removed from their
  shells and chopped
24 clams, steamed, removed from
  their shells and chopped
350g/12oz sweetcorn kernels
350g/12oz long-grain rice, cooked

American

¼ cup butter
1 large onion, chopped
1 garlic clove, crushed
1 green pepper, cored, seeded and
  chopped
1 red pepper, cored, seeded and
  chopped
4 medium tomatoes, skinned, seeded
  and chopped
½ tsp. cayenne
½lb shelled shrimp
24 oysters, shucked and
  chopped
24 clams, steamed, removed from their
  shells and chopped
2¼ cups corn kernels
2 cups long-grain rice, cooked

Melt the butter in a saucepan. Add the onion, garlic and peppers and fry until the onion is golden brown. Stir in the tomatoes, seasoning to taste, cayenne, shrimps, oysters, clams and sweetcorn and cook for 5 minutes, stirring frequently.

Stir in the rice, cover and cook gently for 10 minutes. Serve hot.

SERVES 6-8

Beef bourguignonne

Metric/Imperial	American
45ml/3 tbs. oil	*3 tbs. oil*
1½kg/3lb stewing steak, cubed	*3lb chuck steak, cubed*
1 carrot, sliced	*1 carrot, sliced*
1 onion, sliced	*1 onion, sliced*
25g/1oz flour	*¼ cup flour*
750ml/1¼ pints red wine	*1½ pints red wine*
450ml/¾ pint beef stock	*1 pint beef stock*
3 garlic cloves, crushed	*3 garlic cloves, crushed*
30ml/2 tbs. chopped parsley	*2 tbs. chopped parsley*
18 pickling onions	*18 pearl onions*
½kg/1lb mushrooms, quartered	*1lb mushrooms, quartered*

Preheat the oven to 230°C/450°F, Gas Mark 8.
Heat the oil in a flameproof casserole. Add the beef cubes, in batches, and fry until browned on all sides. Remove the beef cubes from the casserole as they brown. Add the carrot and onion to the casserole and fry until softened. Return the beef cubes, stir in seasoning to taste and sprinkle over the flour, turning over the cubes to coat. Transfer to the oven and cook for 10 minutes. Remove from the oven and reduce the temperature to 170°C/325°F, Gas Mark 3.
Stir in the wine, stock, garlic and parsley and bring to the boil. Cover and return the casserole to the oven. Cook for 2 hours or until the meat is nearly tender. Stir in the onions and cook for a further 30 to 40 minutes. Ten minutes before serving, stir in the mushrooms. Remove the casserole from the oven and transfer the meat and vegetables to a warmed serving platter with a slotted spoon. Put the cooking juices over a high heat and boil rapidly to reduce and thicken them slightly. Strain over the meat and vegetables and serve hot.
SERVES 6-8

Beef carbonnade

Metric/Imperial
1kg/2lb braising steak, cubed
25g/1oz seasoned flour
60ml/4 tbs. oil
6 onions, thinly sliced
2 garlic cloves, crushed
600ml/1 pint dark beer
15ml/1 tbs. brown sugar

American
2lb chuck steak, cubed
¼ cup seasoned flour
¼ cup oil
6 onions, thinly sliced
2 garlic cloves, crushed
2½ cups dark beer
1 tbs. brown sugar

Coat the steak cubes with the seasoned flour. Heat the oil in a saucepan. Add the steak cubes, in batches, and brown on all sides. Remove the steak cubes from the pan as they brown. Add the onions and garlic to the pan and fry gently until softened. Add more oil if necessary. Return the steak cubes to the pan and stir in the beer and sugar. Bring to the boil, then cover and simmer for 1½ hours. Remove the lid and continue simmering for 30 minutes or until the steak cubes are tender. Serve hot. **SERVES 4**

Chinese beef in fruit sauce

Metric/Imperial	American
30ml/2 tbs. oil	*2 tbs. oil*
1 medium onion, thinly sliced	*1 medium onion, thinly sliced*
2 garlic cloves, crushed	*2 garlic cloves, crushed*
2.5cm/1in chopped fresh ginger	*1in piece chopped fresh ginger*
1¼-1½kg/2½-3lb boned leg of beef, cubed	*2½-3lb boneless beef heel of round, cubed*
juice of 1 lemon	*juice of 1 lemon*
juice of 2 oranges	*juice of 2 oranges*
60ml/4 tbs. soy sauce	*¼ cup soy sauce*
300ml/½ pint dry red wine	*1¼ cups dry red wine*
600ml/1 pint water	*2½ cups water*

Preheat the oven to 150°C/300°F, Gas Mark 2.

Heat the oil in a flameproof casserole. Add the onion, garlic and ginger and stir-fry for 1 minute. Add the beef and fry, stirring, for 3 minutes. Stir in the remaining ingredients with seasoning to taste and bring to the boil.

Cover the casserole and place it in the oven. Cook for 4 hours, stirring occasionally.

SERVES 4-6

Daube de boeuf à la Provençale

Metric/Imperial	American
1½kg/3lb stewing steak, cubed	3lb chuck steak, cubed
250g/8oz bacon rashers, cut into strips	½lb bacon slices, cut into strips
250g/8oz mushrooms, sliced	½lb mushrooms, sliced
¾kg/1½lb tomatoes, skinned, seeded and chopped	1½lb tomatoes, skinned, seeded and chopped
3 garlic cloves, crushed	3 garlic cloves, crushed
5ml/1 tsp. grated orange rind	1 tsp. grated orange rind
15ml/1 tbs. chopped parsley	1 tbs. chopped parsley
1 bouquet garni	1 bouquet garni
175ml/6fl oz beef stock	¾ cup beef stock
10 black olives, halved and stoned	10 black olives, halved and pitted

MARINADE	**MARINADE**
300ml/½ pint dry white wine	1¼ cups dry white wine
2.5ml/½ tsp. dried thyme	½ tsp. dried thyme
1 bay leaf	1 bay leaf
2 garlic cloves, crushed	2 garlic cloves, crushed
4 medium onions, sliced	4 medium onions, sliced
4 medium carrots, sliced	4 medium carrots, sliced

Mix all the marinade ingredients together. Add the steak cubes and stir well. Cover and leave to marinate for at least 12 hours, basting occasionally. Remove the beef cubes from the marinade and pat dry with paper towels. Strain the marinade and reserve both the liquid and the vegetables. Discard the bay leaf.

Preheat the oven to 170°C/325°F, Gas Mark 3.

Place two or three bacon strips on the bottom of a flameproof casserole. Spoon a few marinated vegetables, mushrooms and tomatoes on top and cover with a layer of beef cubes. Sprinkle with a little garlic, orange rind and parsley. Add the bouquet garni. Continue making layers in this way, ending with a layer of bacon. Pour in the stock and reserved marinating liquid and scatter over the olives. Bring the liquid to the boil, then transfer to the oven. Cook for 4 hours or until the beef is tender. **SERVES 6-8**

Jamaican casserole

Metric/Imperial

1½kg/3lb stewing steak, cubed
50g/2oz seasoned flour
75g/3oz butter
2 onions, sliced
1 green chilli, seeded and chopped
1 garlic clove, chopped
5ml/1 tsp. ground ginger
400g/14oz canned tomatoes, chopped
2.5ml/½ tsp. dried thyme

American

3lb chuck steak, cubed
½ cup seasoned flour
6 tbs. butter
2 onions, sliced
1 green chili, seeded and chopped
1 garlic clove, chopped
1 tsp. ground ginger
14oz canned tomatoes, chopped
½ tsp. dried thyme

Coat the beef cubes with the seasoned flour. Melt the butter in a large saucepan. Add the beef cubes, in batches, and brown on all sides. Remove the cubes with a slotted spoon. Add the onions, chilli, garlic and ginger to the pan and fry until they are softened. Return the beef to the pan and add the undrained tomatoes and thyme. Bring to the boil. Cover and simmer the mixture for 3 hours or until the beef cubes are tender. Serve hot. **SERVES 6-8**

Pork vindaloo

Metric/Imperial	American
5cm/2in piece chopped fresh ginger	2in piece of chopped fresh ginger
4 garlic cloves, chopped	4 garlic cloves, chopped
7.5ml/1½ tsp. chilli powder	1½ tsp. chili powder
10ml/2 tsp. turmeric	2 tsp. turmeric
6 cloves	6 cloves
2.5ml/½ tsp. ground cardamon	½ tsp. ground cardamon
30ml/2 tbs. coriander seeds	2 tbs. coriander seeds
15ml/1 tbs. cumin seeds	1 tbs. cumin seeds
150ml/5fl oz vinegar	⅔ cup vinegar
1kg/2lb pork fillet, cubed	2lb pork tenderloin, cubed
60ml/4 tbs. oil	4 tbs oil
5ml/1 tsp. mustard seeds	1 tsp. mustard seeds
150ml/5fl oz water	⅔ cup water

Put all the spices and vinegar into a blender and blend to a smooth purée. Add more vinegar if necessary until the mixture forms a liquid paste. Put the pork into a large bowl and mix in the spice paste to coat. Cover and leave to marinate for 1 hour. Transfer to the refrigerator and marinate for 24 hours or overnight, turning occasionally.

Heat the oil in a large saucepan. Add the mustard seeds, cover the pan and cook until they stop spattering. Add the pork, marinade and water and bring to the boil, stirring. Reduce the heat to low and simmer for 40 minutes. Uncover and simmer for a further 30 minutes or until the meat is tender. Serve hot. **SERVES 4-6**

Veal sauté marengo

Metric/Imperial	American
1½kg/3lb lean veal, cubed	3lb lean veal, cubed
100g/4oz butter	½ cup butter
2 medium onions, sliced	2 medium onions, sliced
2 garlic cloves, crushed	2 garlic cloves, crushed
250ml/8fl oz veal or chicken stock	1 cup veal or chicken stock
1 bouquet garni	1 bouquet garni
250g/8oz canned tomatoes, chopped	8oz canned tomatoes, chopped
65g/2½oz tomato purée	¼ cup tomato paste
5ml/1 tsp. paprika	1 tsp. paprika
12 pickling onions	12 pearl onions
350g/12oz button mushrooms, sliced	¾lb button mushrooms, sliced
7.5ml/1½ tsp. flour	1½ tsp. flour

Preheat the oven to 170°C/325°F, Gas Mark 3.

Rub the veal cubes with salt and pepper. Melt half the butter in a flameproof casserole. Add the onions and garlic and fry until softened. Add the veal cubes, in batches, and brown on all sides. Return the veal cubes to the casserole and stir in the stock, bouquet garni, undrained tomatoes, tomato purée (paste) and paprika. Bring to the boil, cover and transfer to the oven. Cook for 1½ hours. Stir in the pickling (pearl) onions, re-cover and cook for a further 30 minutes or until the meat is tender.

Meanwhile, melt 25g/1oz of the remaining butter in a frying pan. Add the mushrooms and fry for 3 minutes, stirring frequently. Transfer the mushrooms to a warmed serving dish.

When the veal is cooked, transfer the veal cubes and pickling (pearl) onions to the serving dish. Keep warm. Strain the cooking liquid into a saucepan and skim off any fat from the surface. Boil until reduced by about one-third. Mix together the remaining butter and the flour to a paste (beurre manié). Add this in small pieces to the liquid and simmer, stirring, until thickened. Pour over the meat and vegetables and serve.

SERVES 6

Osso buco

Metric/Imperial	American
1½kg/3lb veal knuckle, sawn into 7.5cm/3 inch pieces	3lb veal shank, sawn into 3 inch pieces
75g/3oz seasoned flour	¾ cup seasoned flour
100g/4oz butter	½ cup butter
1 large onion, sliced	1 large onion, sliced
400g/14oz canned tomatoes	14oz canned tomatoes
30ml/2 tbs. tomato purée	2 tbs. tomato paste
175ml/6fl oz dry white wine	¾ cup dry white wine
5ml/1 tsp. sugar	1 tsp. sugar
15ml/1 tbs. grated lemon rind	1 tbs. grated lemon rind
2 garlic cloves, crushed	2 garlic cloves, crushed
22.5ml/1½ tbs. chopped parsley	1½ tbs. chopped parsley

Coat the veal pieces with the seasoned flour. Melt the butter in a saucepan. Add the veal pieces, in batches, and fry until browned on all sides. Remove the veal from the pan as it browns. Add the onion to the pan and fry until softened. Stir in the undrained tomatoes, tomato purée (paste), wine, seasoning to taste and sugar and bring to the boil. Return the veal pieces to the pan and mix well. Cover and simmer for 1½ to 2 hours or until the meat is so tender it is almost dropping off the bones.

Meanwhile, mix together the remaining ingredients. Stir into the veal mixture and serve.

SERVES 6

Chicken casserole bonne femme

Metric/Imperial	American
1 x 2kg/4lb chicken	*1 x 4lb chicken*
50g/2oz butter	*¼ cup butter*
¾kg/1½lb pickling onions	*1½lb pearl onions*
¾kg/1½lb small new potatoes	*1½lb small new potatoes*
6 back bacon rashers, diced	*6 Canadian bacon slices, diced*
1 bouquet garni	*1 bouquet garni*

Preheat the oven to 180°C/350°F, Gas Mark 4.

Rub the chicken inside and out with salt and pepper. Melt the butter in a flameproof casserole. Add the chicken and brown lightly on all sides. Remove the chicken from the casserole.

Put the onions, potatoes and bacon in the casserole and cook for 10 minutes, stirring frequently. Return the chicken to the casserole and add the bouquet garni. Cover the casserole and transfer it to the oven. Cook for 45 minutes to 1 hour or until the chicken is tender. Discard the bouquet garni and serve the chicken with the bacon and vegetables. **SERVES 4**

Chicken paprikash

Metric/Imperial

6 chicken quarters
25g/1oz butter
2 large onions, chopped
1 garlic clove, crushed
22.5ml/1½ tbs. paprika
300ml/½ pint chicken stock
2 green peppers, cored, seeded and
  sliced
4 tomatoes, skinned and chopped
22.5ml/1½ tbs. flour
150ml/¼ pint soured cream

American

6 chicken quarters
2 tbs. butter
2 large onions, chopped
1 garlic clove, crushed
1½ tbs. paprika
1¼ cups chicken stock
2 green peppers, cored, seeded and
  sliced
4 tomatoes, skinned and chopped
1½ tbs. flour
⅔ cup sour cream

Rub the chicken pieces with salt and pepper. Melt the butter in a saucepan. Add the onions and garlic and fry until golden brown. Stir in the paprika and cook for a further 2 minutes, then stir in the stock. Add the chicken pieces, peppers and tomatoes to the pan. Cover and simmer for 1 hour or until the chicken is tender. Mix the flour with the sour cream and add to the pan. Cook gently for 2 to 3 minutes, stirring or until the liquid is thickened. **SERVES 6**

Spanish fish stew

Metric/Imperial

150ml/¼ pint olive oil
1 large onion, thinly sliced
250g/8oz squid, cut into rings
6 tomatoes, skinned and chopped
10ml/2 tsp. chopped basil
450ml/¾ pint fish stock
350g/12oz eel, cut into pieces
24 clams, steamed and removed from
  their shells
200g/7oz canned tuna fish, drained
  and flaked
250g/8oz sole fillets, skinned and cut
  into pieces
50g/2oz ground almonds
2.5ml/½ tsp. powdered saffron
2 garlic cloves, crushed
2 slices white bread, fried and
  quartered
8 cooked prawns, unpeeled

American

⅔ cup olive oil
1 large onion, thinly sliced
½lb squid, cut into rings
6 tomatoes, skinned and chopped
2 tsp. chopped basil
2 cups fish stock
¾lb eel, cut into pieces
24 clams, steamed and removed from
  their shells
7oz canned tuna fish, drained and
  flaked
½lb sole fillets, skinned and cut into
  pieces
½ cup ground almonds
½ tsp. powdered saffron
2 garlic cloves, crushed
2 slices white bread, fried and
  quartered
8 cooked jumbo shrimp, unshelled

Heat the oil in a frying pan. Add the onion and fry until it is golden brown. Stir in the squid, tomatoes, basil and quarter of the stock and cook for 3 minutes. Add the eel, clams, seasoning to taste and remaining stock and simmer for 10 minutes. Add the tuna and sole and simmer for a further 10 minutes.

Meanwhile, put the almonds, saffron, garlic, the remaining olive oil and one piece of the fried bread in a mortar. Add 15ml/1 tablespoon of the liquid from the fish mixture and pound together with a pestle to form a paste. Spread the paste on the bottom of a warmed serving dish. Pour the fish mixture into the dish and garnish with the remaining fried bread and the prawns (jumbo shrimp). **SERVES 4-6**

Mediterranean seafood casserole

Metric/Imperial	American
½kg/1lb cod fillets, skinned and cut into 5cm/2in pieces	1lb cod fillets, skinned and cut into 2in pieces
25g/1oz seasoned flour	¼ cup seasoned flour
100g/4oz butter	½ cup butter
2 medium onions, thinly sliced	2 medium onions, thinly sliced
2 garlic cloves, crushed	2 garlic cloves, crushed
200g/7oz canned tuna fish, drained and flaked	7oz canned tuna fish, drained and flaked
100g/4oz mushrooms, sliced	¼lb mushrooms, sliced
1 green pepper, cored, seeded and thinly sliced	1 green pepper, cored, seeded and thinly sliced
400g/14oz canned tomatoes	14oz canned tomatoes
250g/8oz prawns, peeled	½lb shrimp, shelled
250g/8oz frozen scallops, thawed, drained and chopped	½lb frozen scallops, thawed, drained and chopped
250ml/8fl oz dry white wine	1 cup dry white wine
1.25ml/¼ tsp. red pepper flakes	¼ tsp. red pepper flakes
1.25ml/¼ tsp. powdered saffron	¼ tsp. powdered saffron
36 stuffed olives, halved	36 stuffed olives, halved

Preheat the oven to 180°C/350°F, Gas Mark 4.
Coat the fish pieces with the seasoned flour. Melt half the butter in a frying pan. Add the fish pieces, in batches, and brown on all sides. As the fish pieces brown transfer them to a casserole. Add the remaining butter to the pan. When it has melted, add the onions and garlic and fry until softened. Stir in the tuna, mushrooms, pepper, undrained tomatoes, prawns (shrimp) and scallops. Cook for 3 minutes, then stir in the wine, seasoning to taste, red pepper flakes and saffron. Bring to the boil. Stir in the olives and pour over the fish.
Place the casserole in the oven and cook for 20 minutes or until the fish flakes easily.   **SERVES 6**

Boston baked beans

Metric/Imperial	American
1kg/2lb dried haricot beans	*2lb (2¼ cups) dried navy beans*
1 large onion	*1 large onion*
250g/8oz fat salt pork, cubed	*½lb fatback, cubed*
75g/3oz brown sugar	*½ cup brown sugar*
90ml/6 tbs. black treacle	*6 tbs. molasses*
15ml/1 tbs. dry mustard	*1 tbs. dry mustard*

Put the beans in a saucepan with 5ml/1 teaspoon salt and cover with water. Bring to the boil and boil for 2 minutes. Remove from the heat and leave to soak for 1 hour. Return to the heat and bring back to the boil. Half cover the pan and simmer for 30 minutes. Drain the beans.

Preheat the oven to 130°C/250°F, Gas Mark ½.

Put the onion in a casserole. Make a layer of half the beans in the casserole and arrange a layer of half the salt pork chunks on top. Add another layer of beans and finish with the salt pork. Mix together the sugar, treacle (molasses), mustard and seasoning to taste and spoon over the salt pork layer. Pour in enough boiling water to cover. Cover the casserole and place it in the oven. Cook for 5 hours, adding more boiling water when necessary to keep the beans covered. Remove the lid and bake uncovered for a further 45 minutes.

SERVES 6-8

RECIPE INDEX